NEXT LEVEL
LEADERSHIP

WORKBOOK
& DISCUSSION GUIDE

TONY
SUTHERLAND

NEXT LEVEL **LEADERSHIP**
Workbook & Discussion Guide

Tony Sutherland Ministries, Inc.
508 Westwind Way
Atlanta, GA 30107-7720
www.tonysutherland.com

This workbook is the perfect companion to the full 290-page book *UP – Next Level Leadership*. Each chapter in this useful guide corresponds with each chapter in the book. Also, a helpful section containing all the answers is conveniently located at the end to allow for quick reference. This valuable resource will powerfully enhance group discussions as well as personal study.

Contents

CHAPTER 1

A Presence-based Heart

1. The distinctive sign of a church permeated with God's presence is an outpouring of the _____ and manifestations of the _____.

2. The Church is an ethnically and economically diverse community; a radical breed of believers committed to the protection of the unity of the _____, the preserving of the _____ life and the proclamation of the authentic _____ of Jesus.

3. Our ministry platforms are not to raise us up so people can better _____ _____; but so we can better see the _____ _____ we minister to.

4. In order to ignite other hearts for Christ, Christ must first _____ ____.

5. God did not promise to give us acclaimed _____; He promised us to give us _____ after HIS heart.

6. The greatest enemy of the authentic worship of God in our churches is _____ _____.

7. Anyone who wants to be seen as a great leader will probably never be a _____ _____.

8. Godly leaders should not seek to become _____, but rather to become an _____.

9. What man _____ cannot even come close to what God _____.

10. Unless we have valid proof of the presence and power of God, they will remain relatively _____, _____, and _____.

11. One reason for the church's dysfunction is that we have become a church sold out to _____.

12. The church exists for _____ _____, not the pleasure of _____.

13. Any leader that hungers for the _____ of God makes his church eligible to be Presence-based.

14. A passion for God's presence is an attitude we _____. It isn't how we worship, but _____ we worship and _____ we worship.

15. The Presence-based church isn't as interested in attracting _____ as they are attracting _____.

16. The Presence-based church doesn't follow after _____ but after the _____.

17. A church isn't Presence-based by how it plans its _____, chooses its _____, creates sermon _____ or establishes ministries and _____.

18. If we welcome the preeminence of God's invisible presence, the church will be _____.

19. The most distinguishing mark of a Presence-based church is a _____ and _____ to know God as expressed through _____ and _____.

20. In the Presence-based church, worship isn't confined to a _____ _____ service on Sunday morning.

21. Presence-based hearts are compelled to go _____ the _____ to discover the secrets only disclosed in _____.

22. God never _____ His secrets; He only _____ them.

23. God who is so terrifyingly magnificent can be _____ known.

24. The Presence-based church is always pushing past the encounters of _____ and going beyond normal church routine to experience God afresh

25. Our church is a tent but there is _____ _____ within that tent. It is the place we must lead our people.

26. Many of our churches today are experiencing _____ _____.

27. The Church's _____ _____ _____ is to make Jesus Christ and the presence of the Holy Spirit the center of all we are and all we do!

For Discussion:

When was the last time your church experienced a true miracle? What happened? How did it affect the community? Does reliving these events kindle a fire within you?

Do you know people in your community or church that reflect the beliefs expressed in the statistics on page 15 of the book?

Is your church prevailing in your community or is it steadily losing influence? Is your church ready to deliver according to you current marketing efforts? What are you promising those who enter your doors?

Does your church currently foster opportunity for the people to respond after sermons? Describe these moments? How can you optimize these moments to be more efficient and effective?

Give one word that best describes your church. Then add a word to that. Then add another word until you have three words that embody the life of your church.

CHAPTER 2

The Presence-based Church

1. A majority of people who attend Christian worship services leave without feeling that they have _____ God's presence.

2. Eventually people cease to expect a real encounter with God and simply settle for a _____ experience.

3. The word *authentic* is often used to denote that we don't do church the way our _____ did it, and yet is still _____ to produce results.

4. We are living in a culture that is so infatuated with _____ that we have forgotten that the church is about _____.

5. Committed Christians aren't necessarily searching for a new way of _____ _____, but a _____ _____ with the God of their past.

6. This is the Presence-based Church: a community of believers that _____ above all else the

_____ of God's presence and the freedom of the Holy Spirit to move unrestrained.

7. People who understand the power of experiential worship and the genuine move of the Holy Spirit

    (a) They regularly encounter God's _____.

    (b) Their attitudes are conditioned to _____.

    (c) They are constantly built up by God's _____.

    (d) They regularly experience God's _____.

8. Church is a place where we come to get our _____ _____ not get our _____ filled.

9. Many have become all too _____ about approaching God.

10. The Holy Spirit searches the deep and hidden things in our lives that foster an atmosphere where He is either _____ to reign or _____ to move.

11. God has commanded us not to allow the fire in the altar of our lives to _____ _____.

12. The driest church is in the _____ _____ to catch afire with the power and presence of the Holy Spirit.

13. We must not forget the absolute _____ of Jesus and the _____ of the Holy Spirit.

14. The Holy Spirit will _____ _____ of every container we attempt to force Him in and _____ every false image we make of Him.

15. To truly experience the Holy Spirit you cannot sip Him in _____ _____. Rather you must drink of Him freely, fully, _____ and pure.

16. Signs, wonders and the fantastic displays of God's miraculous was absolutely _____ for the full preaching and testimony of the power of the Gospel.

17. The miraculous is never _____. It is always _____ and brings a sense of awe, curiosity and _____.

18. We can always expect the demonstration of the miraculous to _____ the religious conservative.

19. We must not build _____ _____ around God and restrict Him only on an ____ _____basis.

20. The open display of the prophetic power of God witnessed in prophesying, healings, supernatural gifts, and miraculous signs and wonders only MORE GREATLY testifies of the _____ of God to the sinner and believer alike, convincing them of the certainty of His _____.

21. If a move of God is _____, it will bring sinners to their knees and believers to their feet.

22. People are in desperate need to connect with God to _____ what they see, hear, touch and experience among us is truly of Him.

23. It takes a _____ people to help facilitate a genuine move of His Spirit.

For Discussion:

What does authentic community mean to you? Does you church currently reflect that definition? What would it take for your church to become authentic?

Does the ministry of your church services offend the status quo challenge apathy?

Describe your church's approach to worship. Is it too casual? Warm? Reverent? Hurried? Programmed? Do they want to push past the established borders or want it to end sooner?

Does your church tend to cater to the needs of the people and center their services around them? If so, how?

Generally speaking, is your church willing to facilitate and navigate change in the overall dynamic of worship and ministry? Do they want a Presence-based environment? Would they resist the change? Why?

CHAPTER 3

The Presence-based Culture

1. God will not make Himself at home amongst a
   _____ people who refuse to make His presence
   welcomed.

2. The house of God is foremost a place where God's
   presence must be allowed to be on _____
   _____.

3. God is raising up a last days generation with the same
   passion who long to see God's presence restored to its
   _____ _____ and _____.

4. Instead of building an altar and pitching a tent, many
   have chosen to _____ the altar and _____ a
   tent.

5. As leaders in our church services, we spend too much
   time and effort trying to _____ tension,
   _____ to, and _____ people for their
   discomfort and lack of responsiveness

6. Our congregations are a direct reflection of the culture
   we both _____ and _____.

7. If we allow the discomfort of people to _____ the way we develop the culture then we will reap the results.

8. We must boldly lead our people to _____ mountains and _____ fountains.

9. Our people must be taught that the Holy Spirit is in _____ _____.

10. Generally speaking, people fear what they don't _____.

11. Leaders: you are not required to _____ everything you do.

12. Explanation does not always breed _____.

13. Leaders must resist the urge to _____ resistant people.

14. If our opinion of God is too low our response in worship will be _____ to that low opinion.

15. If our people are not worshipping God rightly we don't need to _____ them, we need to help _____ their perspective.

16. We must _____ lead our congregations in love and with great fervor, exhorting them to come out of their _____ and engage God.

17. The Hebrew word for Hallelujah *(Hallal)* means to make a foolish _____, to cause a big _____, to stir up a _____ ruckus and rumpus for our God.

18. Control is a symptom of _____.

19. God is not an _____ _____ in our midst. He's the _____ presiding over all the affairs of HIS house.

20. It is from the _____ _____ _____ where our lives and all great ministry flow.

21. We must recapture a much higher view of God and the mandatory importance of His presence if we are ever to _____ _____ Him.

22. We can't worship these days because we do not have a _____ _____ opinion of God.

23. God's presence is appropriated in our lives in direct relation to our _____ of Him.

24. Our lofty esteem of God will create within us a _____ to make our church services about Him and _____ how we should plan them.

25. We were created to _____ and _____ in the presence of God.

26. The "cool" of God's presence should describe the overall _____ of our church services.

27. We should prefer the _____ of God's presence in our church as opposed to a culturally _____ church.

28. The place of God's presence is the place where we find our _____.

29. When a minister is desperately and passionately committed to the priority of God's presence, he will _____ and have widespread _____.

30. There will always be _____ against the worship of the Church.

31. Don't attempt to build a ministry and _____ God's presence. Build your ministry _____ God's presence!

32. You can build a big _____ without God's presence, but you'll never _____ a generation without it.

33. The problem with building something by your own hand is that it takes the _____ of your _____ _____ to maintain it.

34. When leadership creates ministry structures and programs without the leading of God's presence it is _____ by man's ingenuity.

35. A church thrives in God's _____ _____, when it is built by and overshadowed by the presence of the Lord.

36. Too many churches are more concerned about the signs on display _____ the church instead of the signs on display _____ the church.

37. It is possible to serve God in ministry without the _____ of His presence.

38. You cannot _____ the presence of God

39. The word *manufacture* = _____ + _____ factor.

For Discussion:

What does your church seem to display the most? In practice, does it highlight programs or the presence of God?

If you asked the people in your church to describe the overall tone of your church, what might they say? Visitors? Regular Attendees? Members?

Define the things in your church that put *tension* on the worship? (I.e. people, time elements, programs, announcements, etc.)

How high is the opinion of God amongst the leadership of your church. Is it evident in the life of the church both in ministry, worship, programs and fellowship?

Describe the climate of your church. Is it culturally "cool" or is it "cooled" by the presence of God.

Explain why it is possible to serve God in ministry, without the endorsement of His presence?

CHAPTER 4

Characteristics of a Presence-based Church

1. Man-made systems cannot _____ in the glory of God's real presence.

2. The real cloud of God's glory _____ our direction.

List the **17** characteristics of the presence of God and briefly summarize them (include some scriptures references).

1. _____: _____

_____

_____

2. _____: _____

_____

_____

3. _____: _____

_____

4. _____: _____

5. _____: _____

6. _____: _____

7. _____: _____

8. _____: _____

9. _____: _____

10. _____: _____

_____

_____

11. _____: _____

_____

_____

12. _____: _____

_____

_____

13. _____: _____

_____

_____

14. _____: _____

_____

_____

15. _____: _____

_____

_____

16. _____ : _____

_____

_____

17. _____ : _____

_____

_____

For Discussion:

Describe the type of people that Jesus targeted in His ministry? What is your church's demographic? Are you reaching them?

Does your church put emphasis on being *cool* to reach the culture? Do you feel pressure to be *cool*? What people in your church do you feel you would lose if you placed more priority on God's presence than on image and cultural relevance?

What are the main ministry *pillars* of your church and how do they contribute to the overall sense of God's presence? Do you need to remove some pillars? Add new ones?

Of the 17 characteristics of God's presence in this chapter, which ones does your church exemplify? What characteristics does your church exemplify that are not on this list (good or bad)?

At the end of the day, are your people really impressed with all the programs, marketing, imagery, etc. of your church? What do you feel they want/need the most out of your church services?

CHAPTER 5

Our Need for the Anointing

1. For leaders to thrive in the anointing they must be able to clearly _____ and properly _____ it.

2. For the Kingdom of God to be established and enforced in the earth it requires the _____.

3. The anointing is the supernatural _____, grace and manifested presence of the Holy Spirit operating upon or through an individual or corporate group to produce the _____ of Jesus.

4. We should never use or abuse the anointing in order to _____ _____.

5. God allows us to be _____ under pressure so that we will bring Him glory alone.

6. Trials and tests prepare you for the _____ of His presence to be released though your life.

7. The _____ must never be used for anything else except to bring all honor and glory to God.

8. The anointing is to _____ the power of the Gospel and make _____ _____ famous in the earth.

9. Many who pray for the anointing never receive it because their motive is to use it to their _____ _____.

10. Sometimes a mighty move of God is just plain "_____ _____ _____."

11. Miracles cannot be manufactured by _____ _____.

12. If Jesus was anointed, _____ _____ _____ to think we don't need the same anointing?

13. Many preachers have a lot of *degrees* but they can't bring the _____.

14. Only the anointing can break the _____ _____ _____.

15. The Hebrew word for anointing is _____.

16. We cannot even for a _____ _____ presume to minister without the power of the anointing.

17. A minister that operates in the prophetic is essentially a _____ and _____ of God's mind, heart, words and purpose.

18. For the prophetic ministry, no two meetings are the _____.

19. Another Biblical word for prophet is _____.

20. A seer in the Bible was one who was able to _____ the signs of the times and _____ an undeniably convincing and compelling message based on intensely prayerful _____.

21. Someone who operates in the prophetic is known by others and endorsed by _____ leadership.

22. For the prophetic person, there is often _____ in their tone, demeanor and delivery.

23. The most definable characteristic of a prophetic minister is that he has stood in the _____ _____ _____.

24. _____ is a marked characteristic of the prophetic ministry.

25. A prophetic atmosphere fosters _____.

26. A prophetic atmosphere allows for _____.

27. So many great church services have been _____ between the numbers of a clock.

28. A prophetic atmosphere _____ the Holy Spirit.

29. A prophetic church won't settle for the Holy Spirit's visitation. They crave His _____.

30. A prophetic atmosphere surrenders _____.

31. We are _____ of His presence, not merely service planners or ministry programmers.

For Discussion:

What is your definition of the anointing? How does it differ from the definitions and explanations presented in this book?

How do you know others are anointed? What are the tell tale signs? Do you have to feel something to know others/you are anointed?

Do you feel your church tends to produce (refine and repeat) worship? Does your church's worship, creativity, and ministry methods have a balance of planning and spontaneity?

Does your church incorporate the prophetic in the public context? In Your church services? In your smaller gatherings? How is it incorporated?

CHAPTER 6

A Holy Ghost Outpouring

1. Spirit-filled believers make up the _____ and _____ _____ segment of reformation Christianity in the world.

2. A man who has had an _____ with God is never at the mercy of a _____.

3. While there is an increase of the power and the presence of God in many parts of the world, the Western world of Christianity seems to be _____ or at least _____ from Spirit-filled influence.

4. There is a rise among modern church planters that the spiritual gifts or corporate ministries of the Holy Spirit should not have _____ in public worship today.

5. Spirit-filled ministries must rise up with _____ _____ and _____ to live and minister in the fullness of Holy Ghost Outpouring "outpouring."

6. The Apostle Paul introduced a sense of _____ and _____, but never even slightly _____ the move of the Holy Spirit.

7. Nowhere in Paul's writings, does he even slightly suggest that the manifestations of the Holy Spirit should be _____ from the corporate gathering.

8. Throughout the book of Acts, speaking in tongues in the public setting was not seen as a _____, but as a _____ _____ to unbelievers

9. Speaking in tongues was given by the Holy Spirit to _____ and _____ the indwelling of this gift and as a means of more _____ witness to the non-believing community of the authenticity of the power of God

10. The manifestations of the Spirit of God are a gift not only for personal ministry of the believer but as an agent of _____.

11. God never called the church to _____ itself but rather to be a _____ to attest to the power of God.

12. That which attracts people doesn't necessarily _____ them.

13. Jesus did not tell His disciples that when the power of the Holy Spirit came upon them they would be more _____. He said that they would be _____

14. If there is no evidence in our church services today to give outward witness to this inward indwelling of the Holy Spirit, we will simply appear as _____.

15. We cannot fear that God's way is _____ or _____.

16. Leadership must take _____ _____ of the power at their disposal to draw people to Christ.

17. We must place a _____ _____ on Christ's full anointing on our lives to literally be Jesus to the world.

18. There is a spiritual _____ among people to experience God, and the Church at large must be prepared to offer them what only the Spirit that can _____.

19. The church must refuse to _____ _____ the notion of diluting the power of God in order to attract people.

20. The Holy Spirit was given: to make us bold regardless of _____ or _____.

21. The Holy Spirit was not availed to us for _____, but for _____.

22. The Holy Spirit is a _____ and a _____ to turn the world opposite from satan and directional toward the Savior.

23. The church will only make Christ's presence known when we quit trying to use other _____ _____

24. The Holy Spirit is not a tool _____ _____ for our benefit. It's a tool that _____ _____ for His benefit and His glory.

For Discussion:

Describe a significant encounter with God you have had that would make people skeptical?

Before reading this book, did you feel that the manifestations of the Holy Spirit were not for public context? How do you feel now?

Is speaking in tongues an experience that you have had? Never had? Want to have? Want others to have? Not sure? Fearful?

On question number 17, what does *"place a desperate demand on Christ's full anointing"* mean to you?

What are some of the *"other methods"* that get in the way of the church making Christ's presence known?

CHAPTER 7

Discerning the Excesses

1. The tell tale sign that the Spirit is truly working on and in someone's life is the _____ and _____ that they carry about on a regular basis.

2. If someone is genuinely moving in the things of God they will demonstrate _____ in their personal character and relationships.

3. Some people are so hungry for revival and an outbreak of the supernatural that they would rather _____ _____ or _____ it than not have it at all.

4. According to Jesus, "evil and adulterous" people have _____ only for the *signs* rather than the One who gives the signs.

5. We veer into spiritual _____ when we look for benefits from something that we don't have real _____ with.

6. If Satan can _____ the quality of a move of God by sending the false, he can successfully restrict and limit the effectiveness of the true move of God.

7. We don't look to _____. Rather we look to _____.

8. Signs from God are always meant to make Jesus Christ the _____ _____.

9. We know a sign is from God because of the _____ _____ of the Holy Spirit that searches the mind and heart of Christ within us.

10. We must be mature in the _____ ____ _____ and armed with knowledge and wisdom. Satan loves to prey on simple minds.

11. The plan of the enemy is to _____ God's reality, _____ ministries, and turn people away from the Faith.

12. The problem with living by signs is they can be _____ _____. They can come from the wrong _____.

13. Signs are meant to keep us _____ _____ our destination. They are not meant for us to stop, build shrines and dance around them.

14. There are _____ and _____ _____ that are not from the Lord.

15. Certain signs are placed in the road to _____ us from our destination. We mustn't allow ourselves be _____ or distracted by them.

16. Just because a sign may be _____, doesn't mean the sign is from God or that it's pointing you to God.

17. God isn't the only one _____ _____ on the road.

18. There are two common elements to everything God does: The _____ of His Word and the _____ of Jesus.

19. God's responses and displays of power are always in line with His _____.

20. God's Word and presence will always bring _____ _____ in the lives of people.

21. A true miracle _____ _____.

22. A true miracle originates from a _____ _____.

23. One of the gifts of the Spirit is the _____ ____ _____ that enables us to distinguish between true and false spirits.

24. The Holy Spirit Himself dwells within all believers, and through His eyes, a true sign, wonder or miracle can be _____.

25. No matter how convincing a sign may appear, if it _____ people from glorifying God, is _____ in nature, causes _____ or creates a feeling of _____, it should be discerned as a demonic diversion.

26. A true miracle stands the test of _____ _____.

27. A true miracle _____ _____ _____.

28. The teaching and preaching of the Word of God, accompanied by the miracles of God, work in _____ _____ for the full proclamation of the gospel.

For Discussion:

Have you truly ever met someone who is passionate about God's presence and supernatural manifestations, yet seemed "shady?"

Do you know any Spirit-filled people who genuinely love God and others and reflect integrity in their character and relationships?

Have you ever experienced spiritual manifestations of such a nature that it frightened you? Convinced you? What were the differences between the two?

Describe a truly authentic supernatural occurrence that convinced you of the Holy Spirit's Power and of the Lordship of Jesus Christ. What convinced you?

CHAPTER 8
The Last Days Church

1. God did not call worship leaders to be _____ _____ using their platforms to show off their next new worship _____.

2. The true last days church will not grow in _____ but rather will be a constant, _____ _____ to lovers of the flesh and the world.

3. Jesus said the whole world would _____ us because of His name.

4. It is _____ for the church to earn the world's _____.

5. The only way to earn acceptance from the world is to _____ the message of Christ and _____ the power of Christ.

6. The heat of _____ is rising amongst Christians as is evident in the media and in politics and will only _____ in the coming days.

7. Nowhere in the Bible does it speak of a _____ _____ church.

8. The Bible explicitly prophesies of a LAST DAYS church characterized by _____, _____, _____ and a pouring out of His _____ on all mankind.

9. Not only should we be *seeker sensitive,* we must be even more so _____ _____ after God.

10. Signs and wonders must accompany the salvation message in order that the power of God can be _____.

11. MIRACLES were given to the church to endorse the _____ of the church.

12. Many churches pull the *seeker sensitive* card as an excuse to _____ _____ their worship services

13. God did not call us as leaders to _____, _____ or _____ _____ to the nonchalant and passionless churchgoer.

14. In these last days, the church needs leaders who are _____ with the status quo.

15. In the last days church young leaders will arise with a deep prophetic urgency of God's heart and a clear _____ of His _____ for their times.

16. This Last-Days *select* has an innate sensitivity towards spiritual _____, _____ and _____.

17. Last Days leaders have a _____ spirit but remain true to moral _____ and ancient _____.

18. Real church leadership intentionally and strategically _____ with popular culture, but only with great trepidation, steadfastly _____ its charms.

19. Last days leaders are not _____ chasers; they are _____ chasers.

20. Anyone who dares _____ the call to revolution will do so in the face of _____.

21. The Last Days church will _____ and _____ _____ the wisdom and leadership of the elderly and spiritually mature.

22. Modern day leaders tend to go after a _younger_ demographic, leaving the _____ to blend into the landscape.

23. When you isolate yourself from the wisdom of the past you rage against all _____ _____ for the future.

24. In the last days church an explosive demonstration of the _____ will be unleashed.

25. The Holy Spirit is our _____ or _____ _____ to the promise of Jesus' presence.

26. Many church services today have a great deal of drama but no real _____; a lot of bells and whistles but no real _____ _____.

27. During great darkness in the world, God's glory will be _____ upon the church! The darker the world becomes the _____ the church will _____.

28. In the last days political leaders and world governments will _____ to the _____ for answers and direction!

29. World leaders will seek out men and women of God who show evidence of having been in the _____ of God.

30. We must not recant on _____ _____ and spiritual directives merely to gain acceptance and open audience with world leaders. Boldness must increase where opportunity is _____.

31. In the last days church exponential _____ and _____ will be normal and increase with great momentum.

32. In the last days church the gospel of _____ will spread _____.

33. The gospel of the Kingdom is the message of
    _____.

34. Jesus promised us that if HE be _____,
    _____ and _____ then He would draw all
    men from every nation, tribe and tongue to Him.

35. The last days church will be a church of unstoppable
    _____.

For Discussion:

Do you see a trend in the church to be accepted by the world?

Is the church using its opportunity to be an influence to the world or famous in the world?

Is church is trying more methods of marketing or contending for more miracles? What are the obvious signs?

As a leader, are you prepared to give sound counsel to world leaders (i.e. Daniel, Joseph)? Do you provide a platform in your church to connect with regional government leaders? Discuss you could take to make this happen?

How is your church pulling on the wisdom past leadership to help create, administrate and functionally navigate the vision and mission of your church?

CHAPTER 9
The Personality Driven Church

1. God's system of leadership is the _____ _____ model.

2. We should build ministries and churches not to get us discovered but get Jesus _____.

3. In the personality-driven environment, the church is not a true community; rather it's a _____ _____.

4. A truly healthy church body naturally grows because it is nurtured by a community of pastoral _____.

5. Sadly, many times leaders reject the servant-leadership concept because it is too _____.

6. Would you be content to give up all notoriety and _____ _____ _____ to see God's glory revealed and His purposes come to pass in the lives of others?

7. True shepherds smell like their _____.

8. Real pastors are touchable, personable and can be found abiding amongst the people they lead slowly _____ _____ _____.

9. If you want to be a BIG leader, you're going to have to stay _____.

10. Leadership is _____.

11. In the personality driven model, the leader is at the top and all the people below _____ _____ _____.

12. In the Servant-Leadership Model the leader considers himself the _____ and serves the needs of others _____.

13. Servant-leaders are rare because of the level of _____ required.

14. If it's your desire to be seen as great _____ _____, then you have the wrong motivation and will never be seen as great among men.

15. The human condition is _____ _____ by God to worship and will automatically fashion an idol when the authentic is _____.

16. Personalities are those we see _____ _____.

17. The word of the prophet is never _____.

18. _____ _____ systems that are doomed to fail

19. Too often we replace THE King with _____ _____.

20. So many leaders do things that that God never intended because of the _____ of the people.

21. Be careful not to sellout to the world lest you _____ _____ _____ of God's purposes.

22. Top leaders should never _____ _____ for what others do for them

23. The quality people most admire in a man is his _____.

24. Jesus did not come to be _____, but to _____.

25. Jesus didn't rule his disciples with an _____ _____. He ruled them with an _____ _____.

26. As you develop people into the leaders they are to become, they will in turn become your most _____ _____.

27. Invest greatly into your leaders as if they are preparing to _____ _____ for their own God-given destiny.

28. A _____ or an _____ is a leader who pretends he believes in his team but has ulterior motives.

29. You will never be short of great leaders if you believe in and develop the _____ _____ _____.

30. Authentic leaders treat others with _____,
_____ _____.

31. The presence of Jesus is never a _____ to be
traded for our institutional presence in the _____.

For Discussion:

Does marketing your church and its programs truly and ultimately lead to people discovering Christ?

What are some of the costs and sacrifices associated with true servant-leadership?

Does your leadership reflect kindness? Frustration? Forcefulness? Aggravation? Distance? Coldness? What are the contributing factors to these?

Does your church apply the traditional concept of leading with and "iron fist" or an "open hand"?

How is your church pulling on the wisdom past leadership to help create, administrate and functionally navigate the vision and mission of your church?

Would you consider your church a place where people will hear what God is saying regardless if it's popular or not? Do you feel your congregation only wants to hear messages that inspire them? Challenge them? Both?

Are you afraid to invest too much into your leaders for fear they will abandon you for the next big thing?

CHAPTER 10

Presence-based Leadership

1. God did not call us to _____ with the world but to _____ _____.

2. Presence-based leaders are forged on the _____ _____ _____.

3. God must have a leader He can _____ to boldly declare the _____ and delicately facilitate His _____.

4. Ambitious and driven leaders must be _____, _____ and _____ as not to make ministry about them but about _____.

5. Godly leadership isn't about what we're building but about whom we're _____.

6. Ambitious leaders quickly shun certain assignments thinking that God could not possibly be in anything _____.

7. Most spiritual leaders will never be _____.

8. God is not looking for success. He's simply looking for
   _____.

9. Many times, when we do what God tells us, it doesn't
   _____ how we thought it would.

10. We will never truly know what our obedience meant in
    this life until we see it from _____ _____.

11. When we learn to _____ the process of God, we are
    enabled to _____ the purpose of God.

12. The anointing of God isn't just so we'll have great
    power for ministry but that we'll be able to endure the
    _____ of ministry.

13. Becoming a great man or woman of God isn't in what
    you've learned to do but in what you've learned to
    _____ .

14. In order to become a spiritual giant, you will have to
    face many _____ along the way.

15. It's amazing what a leader can accomplish for the
    Kingdom of God when he's not concerned about
    _____ for his part in the process.

16. There are no _____ for Presence-based leaders.
    Shortcuts cut a leader's effectiveness <u>short</u>.

17. As a Presence-based leader you will feel like an
_____.

18. _____ _____ is normal for those who have
been called into ministry.

19. Your assignment is both your _____ and your
_____.

20. A Presence-based leader will be treated _____.

21. Becoming a leader will reveal your _____ _____.

22. When the enemy wants to overthrow you he'll
_____ someone _____ you.

23. Some people enter your life to be a _____ while
others enter your life to be a _____.

24. Not every difficult person is from the _____.

25. Critics keep us _____.

26. Presence-based leaders are forced to _____.

27. Godly promotion is often _____, _____,
_____ and even at times severely _____.

28. A Presence-based leader's heart will be painfully
_____.

29. Many leaders prostitute Christ's bride. They use her for their _____. God will not have a leader like this.

30. Don't mistake meekness with _____.

31. The perplexity of our trials is like a double-edged razor that prunes the _____ ____ _____ off of us.

32. Heart circumcision prevents us from accepting glory and keeps the attitude of _____ at bay.

33. Heart circumcision keeps promotion from going to our _____!

For Discussion:

Describe some of your "anvils of adversity" in ministry and how they forged you? What did you learn?

Who are some of the people you are raising in your assignment? Do you see the greatness in them or do you see the greatness in yourself for raising them?

How does obscurity sound to you? If God so chooses, are you willing to never be discovered in order that He receives all the glory? Be honest?

Have you or anyone you've ever known been promoted but it didn't look that way? Explain.

CHAPTER 11

Performance-based Leadership

1. We cannot make up for the lack of true spiritual power with our _____, _____ and _____.

2. Miracles caused the early Christians to _____ and sinners to _____.

3. Only the power and demonstration of the gospel can hold people _____.

4. To _____ means to think, ponder and to creatively imagine.

5. To _____ means to keep busy by means of entertainment, thus clouding our ability to think, reason and make sound judgment.

6. Only real worship is _____ and acceptable to God.

7. Leaders cannot rely on their _____ _____ to manipulate people.

8. When we try to put *our hand* in the oil of anointing we end up _____ Jesus.

9. Worship leaders often rely too much on _____ to pull off the *illusion* of worship.

10. We must be careful not to become too preoccupied with our creativity that we forget about the _____.

11. God's power trumps the _____ every time!

12. When we attempt to lead worship with fleshly devices, we are dabbling in the _____.

13. Presence-based leaders seek to minister from a place of _____, _____, _____ and _____.

14. Presence-based leaders _____ in the real move of God and _____ in cultural relevance.

15. Presence based leaders refuse to be _____ and make _____ in their convictions.

16. Presence-based leaders are willing to skip _____ to get to the punch of God's outpouring.

17. Although Presence-based leaders use creativity to enhance the _____, they are careful not to augment the _____.

18. Jesus is the _____ of all Presence-based activity.

19. Presence-based leaders love people and use _____ versus loving things and using _____.

20. _____ cannot be packaged, boxed, shrink-wrapped or perforated. Jesus is not a product. He's a person.

21. Presence-based leaders refuse to _____ the move of God.

22. Presence-based leaders effectively steward both _____ and _____ methods of ministry.

23. Presence-based leaders aren't _____ or _____ by modern culture.

24. Presence-based leaders are _____ with mediocrity and apathy yet without _____.

25. Presence-based leaders do not tolerate _____ to the Holy Spirit in their lives.

26. The _____ _____ _____ fills Presence-based leaders' thoughts and conversations

27. Presence-based leaders refuse to be _____, but rather walk in a _____ _____ for others.

28. Presence-based leaders live on the edge of expectancy for an _____ of God's manifest Spirit.

29. Presence-based leaders are often _____ and perceived as overboard or _____ _____.

For Discussion:

Describe how amusement has the ability to sap our ability to deeply ponder and press into the presence of God? Do you think the church allows for too much entertainment as to amuse?

Explain how worship is undeniable. What are some qualities or characteristics in corporate worship that reflect undeniable worship? Is it difficult to put in words? Why?

How do we "put our hand in the anointing oil" of Christ's presence?

Have you or anyone you've ever known been promoted but it didn't look that way? Explain.

Have you or anyone you've ever known been promoted but it didn't look that way? Explain.

Can you recall a time when the Holy Spirit was about to move in a special way in your church but leadership chose NOT to forgo what they was planned? Describe how you felt. Were you frustrated? Disappointed? Angry? Confused? Relieved?

Can you recall a time when the Holy Spirit was about to move in a special way in your church and leadership chose TO forgo what they was planned? Describe how you felt. Were you frustrated? Disappointed? Angry? Confused? Relieved?

CHAPTER 12

Image Driven Ministry

1. Image-driven ministry patterns, markets, targets and packages itself to a _____ _____ and culture.

2. Presence-based leaders have a _____ _____ consciousness, embracing and preferring people of all shapes, sizes, colors, fashions, ages, etc.

3. Presence-based leaders resemble God's _____ _____ _____.

4. Performance-based leaders feel they have no prerogative but to "confront" or even dismiss people when they fall into either of these categories: _____, _____ and out of _____.

5. Jesus didn't target a _____.

6. Jesus not only came to win the _____ and save the _____.

7. We need to quit finding reasons for dismissing people in ministry and discover reasons why we should _____ _____ _____ and why Christ would keep them involved.

8. In Bible times, the elderly, grey haired, apostle was most _____ and _____. They were the _____ leaders of their time.

9. In the Last Days church the young and old _____ _____.

10. The Last Days church is a _____ church, both young and old marching side by side, ministering off of each other's strengths fostered in a culture where mutual _____ and _____ is forged.

11. We cannot assume to tell people their time is up if they are legitimately struggling with certain issues regarding their appearance and yet have a powerful _____ ____ _____ upon their life.

12. Ministers need to spend less time on their _____ and more time in their _____.

13. To cut people out of leadership because of age and physical standards is to _____ Christ's own precious body.

14. No matter how we look, we're loved and considered beautiful and valuable to God and should be treated no less by church leadership when it comes to _____ _____ _____.

15. We mustn't apply _____ _____ to the picture-perfect beauty of Christ's bride. We're called to let her _____ in all her glorious imperfections.

16. God is teaching older ministers to _____ _____ in their transitions as He prepares them for _____ _____ in their next assignment.

17. When we start out in ministry, most of us assume we'll do what we're doing for the rest of our lives. However, It doesn't always _____ that way.

18. God wants us to be a _____ _____ in the lives of so many coming up.

19. _____ _____ need us to love them, believe in them encourage them, and speak wisdom into their future.

20. For God to use any of us, He must _____ _____ _____, including fear, self-doubt, jealousy, disappointment and regret.

21. Presence-based leaders need to be molded at _____ _____, not just when we're young.

22. Embrace the transitions of your life _____. Believe that God has amazing things for you that you would've _____ _____ had He told you.

23. Your most fruitful days are _____ _____!

24. It's not mainly about _____ or what YOU do. It's about who _____ and what HE'S doing IN you!

25. If we truly desire to be Presence-based leaders that God can use for entire the span of our lifetime, we must be reminded at every stage in life and ON every *stage* in ministry that it's _____ _____ _____!

For Discussion:

When you look at the ministry platform does it resemble God's glorious melting pot? Older generation? Younger generation? Multi generational?

What demographic does your church target? Worship ministry target? Have you considered what you will do ten to twenty years from now as a church? Will your target be any different?

Is there an over/under emphasis on fashion, physical fitness among your leadership? Does your church focus too much on appearance and fashion in ministry? Does it embarrass you to see people out of style? How do you think God feels?

Is there a 'disconnect' with older people in your church? Are they avidly and regularly involved? If someone in their fifties came to audition for the worship team would they be allowed to participate and even stand on the front line of worship?

CHAPTER 13

Confronting the 'Me' Monsters

Ambition • Promotion • Envy • Rejection

1. In a leader's life it's all about _____.

2. You will never rise above the level of your _____.

3. Major failures are nothing more than ignoring the
   _____ _____ over a significant season of time.

4. The Presence-based leader cherishes the _____
   _____ of God above all else.

5. The self-seeking leader does whatever it takes to get to
   the top, regardless of what it _____ or who it _____.

6. The self-seeking leader looks for ladders to _____
   while the servant-leader _____ the ladder for others.

7. Be careful what doors you kick down. There are
   _____ _____ waiting on the other side.

8. God tests your _____ more than anything else.

9. Don't get drunk on your own _____.

10. Don't believe your own _____ _____.

11. If you're too _____ to stand on the small stage, you're too _____ to stand on the big stage.

12. Whenever you promote yourself you take an _____ _____ from God to do it _____ _____.

13. Our boasting must be in _____ _____.

14. Swagger is the dagger that _____!

15. God uses _____, _____ and _____ to temper selfish ambition.

16. Any promotion you politic for can be _____ from you.

17. Humble yourself and you'll eventually be _____. Promote yourself and you'll eventually be _____.

18. Promotion offers more and greater _____ but it also presents more and greater _____.

19. Some will be _____ by your promotion. Flaunt it and you'll be _____ even more. (i.e. Joseph)

20. You delay promotion when you share your _____ with the wrong people

21. _____ is often the best protector of dreams.

22. Sometimes promotion doesn't feel like _____.

23. If promotion isn't that important to you, then you're probably _____ for promotion.

24. Whatever you're willing to surrender you're more prepared to _____.

25. Don't chase applause, fame or money. Become the best version of yourself and those things will eventually _____ _____!

26. The anointing is exclusively reserved for _____.

27. When you serve, trust that you are _____ regardless of your _____.

28. It is in the crucible of serving where we eventually learn to let go of our _____.

29. God _____ those who serve Him with their whole heart.

30. We are _____ in God's house.

31. The way to the Throne Room is through the _____ _____.

32. Humility is not a _____; it's a _____.

33. Envy is a _____ _____.

34. Envy causes you to betray the _____.

35. Envy _____ you to your own promise and potential.

36. When we compare ourselves to others, we betray our own _____.

37. When you envy others successes you reject God's _____ and accuse Him of _____.

38. When you envy others you reject the unique and significant thing the Holy Spirit is _____ in YOUR life.

39. Envy prevents you from being _____.

40. Envy is a _____ spirit.

41. Don't fall for the lie that God has run out of _____ and there's none left for you.

42. Don't envy other's _____. You have no idea what _____ they've had to endure to get there.

43. When you despise the God-given success of others you despise _____ _____.

44. Rejection is _____.

45. Most people are _____ more than they're
_____.

46. We come to better understand and embrace God's
acceptance only as we are purified in the _____
_____ _____ _____.

47. Rejection is 5 things: _____, _____, not
_____, _____, _____.

48. Rejection is God's divine _____ not His
_____.

49. Your enemies actually serve as a _____ _____
towards your promotion.

50. When people throw *bricks* at you they supply
_____ _____ for your dream.

51. Your haters only make you _____!

For Discussion:

What are some small things that people tend to ignore that end
up causing major failures?

Have you ever been intoxicated by your own achievements and suffered for it? Share your experience. How did you learn from it and apply it the next time around?

How does "swagger" cause you to fall prey to the devices of the enemy?

Do you feel anointed when you serve? Do you believe God is mightily using you when you don't feel it?

Have there ever been times when you served in ministry that it felt like you going through the motions?

When was the last time you secretly celebrated the failure of someone? Did it help cure your envy? If you struggle with envy share some of the ways you have learned to overcome it.

Do you ever feel God has run out of favorable opportunities for you when you see others succeed?

How has rejection made you life better in the long run? How have your haters made you greater?

Out of the four 'me' monsters, what are the hardest you've ever had to regularly wrestle with: Ambition, Promotion, Envy, or Rejection?

CHAPTER 14

A Culture of Excellence

1. Excellence is in the very essence, nature and character of God. Whenever His name is mentioned, _____ is ascribed.

2. A Presence-based church is not _____ in excellence because God is not _____ in it.

3. Presence-based leader's commitment to excellence is _____ than the average church.

4. Although Presence-based leaders are not willing to sacrifice character and consecration, they accept ____ _____ than the best.

5. The presence of God does not promote an attitude of _____ nor excuse _____.

6. A culture of excellence should distinguish the Presence-based environment from even the _____ of church leadership models.

7. Many leaders avoid promoting a move of God in their churches for fear that excellence will be totally _____.

8. A Presence-based ministry should always be _____ because Jesus is at the center of it.

9. Presence-based ministry should have greater influence and more dynamic impact because it possesses the ideals _____ embraces.

10. By definition *excellence is the state or attitude of excelling or being exceptionally _____; having extreme _____ and displaying superior _____.*

11. Excellence is having the mindset to <u>excel</u>, to achieve _____, to always be on the _____ of being wise and faithful to maximize our _____.

12. Excellence is doing the _____ with what you have.

13. A person of excellence never stops _____.

14. God's presence _____ excellence at every level.

15. God wants His church to _____ Him well.

16. We must make the absolute best _____ we can in designing our facilities and planning our services.

17. From the moment people walk onto our campus they should say, "_____!"

18. God wants His presence and our presence in the community to be simultaneously _____.

19. We should make every effort to make God's house and His praise _____.

20. Every time we do something in the church it should _____ the excellent ministry of Jesus.

21. We must always reach _____ when representing His greatness to our world.

22. All of our activity surrounding the life of the church, should be done so with such excellence that the world will _____ _____.

23. When people see us as a living demonstration of Jesus in every facet, they will inevitably be _____ to Him.

24. God doesn't want to be introduced as the most _____ or _____ person in the world.

25. We should make plans to go _____ for the gospel.

26. Excellence raises the level of your _____ and _____.

27. Quality attracts _____.

28. Nominally minded people attract the _____ _____ of people.

29. A good test of leadership is to turn around and look at the people who are _____ _____.

30. There's absolutely nothing wrong with a Godly and healthy desire to ____ _____ _____.

31. Mediocre people always ask _____ They are satisfied with _____ _____ _____.

32. People of Excellence have a _____ ____ _____ attitude. They're mantra is "It's _never_ _good_ _enough._"

33. The top 3 qualities of People of Excellence are Excellence of _____, _____ and _____.

34. According to 1 Samuel 16:18, to get a "call" from the King you must: Possesses God given _____, Strive for _____, Walk in _____, Maintain good _____, Radiate God's _____ and Carry the _____.

35. The most important qualification that trumps all else in a leader's life is the _____ of God's presence in his life and ministry.

36. We can actually possess God given abilities and yet the presence of the Lord may not necessarily _____ us.

37. We must always feel a sense of _____ without God.

38. It's not so much about God giving us more, but rather trusting God to do _____ through our _____.

For Discussion:

What has been your traditional view of excellence? After studying this chapter do you have a differing view?

Have you always been and advocate of excellence? Has it been very important, relatively important, not important?

Does your church and leadership reflect the excellence that is worthy of God's name and His presence?

What are some areas in your ministry that reflect top quality? What needs improvement?

If a visitor would visit you church this coming Sunday, what would they say? How would they feel?

Revisit question #38. Do you feel that this is plausible?

CHAPTER 15

A People of One Thing

1. Many are weary of being a _____ _____ but only an _____ _____.

2. If we have no sense of God's _____, we either stop _____ or pursue the _____ _____ altogether

3. David's one consuming passion was to _____ the face of God.

4. The Bible teaches us five ways to pursue a move of God: We are to: _____, _____ ourselves, _____ His face, _____, and _____.

5. We should always be on the _____ for traces of His presence in our lives, ministries and our churches.

6. _____ is the key to discovery.

7. Humbling ourselves involves knowing that we are utterly _____ without God.

8. Being a Presence-based church doesn't mean we need five hour worship services. It means sensing God's presence in a powerful way in the _____ _____.

9. When the atmosphere is latent with a hunger for God, His presence will be recognized in the _____ _____ _____.

10. We need to learn to be comfortable with the spontaneous and willing to _____ from the plan.

11. Pride says, *"Don't look* _____ *or* _____ _____ _____ *at all costs."*

12. Often our level of hunger for God will determine whether or not we're _____ to the move of God.

13. We must let Jesus invade our _____ _____.

14. Seeking God's face not only means looking for Him for everything; it also means to _____ Him with our whole heart.

15. We must learn as individuals and churches to *press* into God's presence: to _____ pursue the move of God not just _____ for it.

16. Worship is not a _____ _____ or a _____ _____ to the service. We must learn to open our hearts to more than just a performance of songs.

17. Passion moves God's heart, which in turn moves the _____ ____ _____.

18. Passionate prayer is the _____ _____ of the church.

19. God responds to _____.

20. Our prayers _____ our true desires and if our desires are _____ _____ with His will and for His glory, He answers accordingly.

21. A people of grace live a lifestyle of _____.

22. The Greek word for *repentance* means to _____ _____ _____.

23. To repent doesn't mean to _____ in your sin or waywardness. It involves _____ to the priorities of the Kingdom of God.

24. Repentance is both _____ the Gospel (Good News of Jesus) and _____ from our sin

25. God is not looking for a _____ church. He's looking for a _____ church: a church that is willing to change its course.

26. When the church veers off course we should _____, _____ around and _____ to our priority.

27. We should not feel _____ in sin or rebellion to God.

28. Repentance always has to do with _____.

29. When the _____ on Jesus and the _____ for holiness is missing; the move of God will be _____.

For Discussion:

Are you regularly aware of God's presence throughout the day? Explain.

How long does it usually take you church during any particular worship service to sense God's presence corporately? Individually? What do you think is the key or hindrance?

Do you feel your worship services are more like warm ups or pre shows to the main event?

Do you think God answers prayer or right desire? The answer to this question may enlighten you to how your prayers may more effectively and frequently be answered.

In light of the meaning of repentance (change your mind) what does a lifestyle of repentance mean?

CHAPTER 16

The Vice Versus of Ministry

1. The vice versus in ministry are:

   Be about one thing vs. many _____.

   Please God vs. pleasing _____.

   Seek God's hand vs. seeking His _____.

   Be known in Heaven & hell vs. being known on _____.

   Know the power of truth vs. the truth about _____.

   Wasting your life vs. wasting your _____.

   Move God vs. moving _____.

   Embrace extravagance vs. maintaining _____.

   Build a house for God vs. a house for _____.

2. What is the point of being a people of one thing? What do we gain?" _____ _____!

3. Someone who seeks God's face and longs to touch His heart will never be satisfied with a _____ _____ _____ of songs.

4. We shouldn't only seek God's hand but more so, His _____.

5. Why would God give us things if those things will be used for _____ _____?

6. The Giver is far better than His _____.

7. At the end of the day God's presence is always better than just His _____.

8. When people see that we have REAL influence with the _____ ____ _____, they will raise their eyebrows and take notice.

9. We must quit trying to impress our community with _____ and _____ and seek to make a powerful spiritual impression upon them.

10. We must contend for miracles more than we do for _____ or _____.

11. We desperately need a fresh outpouring of _____ _____ to cast out demons, heal the sick, restore relationships and comfort broken people.

12. People are weary of sermons about the _____ ____ _____.

13. We need to rethink the _____ _____. Are we really missing something so life changing that church is a waste of time to us?

14. Anything more important to us than a _____ _____
    _____ is truly a waste of our lives.

15. When we move the heart of God, the impact will ring
    through the _____.

16. Worship is extravagant _____ and extreme _____.

17. Yesterday's radical is today's _____.

18. In our sincere attempts to _____ _____ we've
    almost made them the center of attention instead of
    God's presence.

19. We shouldn't build a house and invite God's presence.
    We build a house _____ God's Presence.

20. In the "seeker sensitive" movement, worship tends to
    center on the needs of the _____ rather than the
    One being _____.

21. True Biblical Worship is defined as the _____
    _____ _____, not ourselves.

22. We don't _____ _____ simply because we don't
    truly know the God of the Bible.

23. Until the theology of Christ is restored to its proper
    place through a new reformation, our "nonchalantness"
    will never be _____.

24. _____ is the careful, fervent, and reflective view about God.

25. We should strive to minister in the vocabulary and style of shifting trends while steering clear of adopting a _____ _____ _____ of God.

26. Asphyxiated souls don't need _____ _____. They need an _____ _____.

27. Do we want to simply settle for putting a _____ on people's faces or do we desperately want to help make a _____ in their hearts.

28. By and large, most people don't read the Bible. And because they don't read it, we have become a nation of _____ _____.

29. Studies also show that many post moderns between the ages of 16-29 want more out of church than just a _____ _____. They want a faith that promotes a return to true Biblical Christianity.

30. Church is not the imagery we design, a package we _____ or a service we _____. It is a Person we _____!

31. Sadly, the chant of many churchgoers today is, "We _____, we _____, we _____." But what about We _____?

32. We must not fear the discomfort of _____ _____ for being a people passionately and radically after God's heart.

33. We must press into the things of God knowing that the devil will _____ _____.

For Discussion:

Have you ever heard the statement "What's the point of all of this?" in regards to church services? If so, give specifics. How did it make you feel? Did you agree? Disagree?

How would you classify your worship services more about getting God to do things or simply dwell among you? What is the difference between the two and what has a better result?

In question #10 what does "contend for miracles" mean to you? How would you implement this in your personal prayer life and the life of the church? Do we settle for no miracles since we don't see them that often?

Do you or somebody you know fit into the category of yesterday's radical? How have you changed? What will you do about it?

Do you feel a majority of your church fits into the classification of Biblical illiteracy? What can you do to instigate change?

CHAPTER 17

A Revival People

1. God always had a _____ _____ through every church age.

2. The history of the church and its ongoing expansion is absolutely dependent upon _____ _____.

3. Everyday, _____ men and women seeking after God, changed and even created the chronicles of history with their lives, their prayers and their fervor.

4. God is still looking for a revival people. History is not _____ and neither is God.

5. You are a direct result of someone's _____, _____ and _____.

6. You can still play a _____ role in changing history.

7. True revival is a means that always serves towards the of the _____ ___ _____.

8. Revival is sparked by and marked by an increase of _____ _____ that distinguishes it from normal and nominal church as usual.

9. It is entirely possible to _____ and even _____ revival in the life of the church.

10. The Holy Spirit is ultimately _____, _____ and _____ _____ _____ every revival

11. Passion and desire ultimately serve to help the church at large _____, _____, and _____ revival together.

12. All of church history is one harmonious display of God's _____ _____ linked to and flowing into the next move.

13. Revival is not a term describing simply winning the lost nor is it the shifting of political environments. These are the _____ of revival.

14. To revive means to bring something back to life, _____ that which was _____ _____.

Four things that happen to a church that is revived:

• The church _____ of its sins as it becomes _____ _____ of God's presence and His extraordinary works.

• The church experiences a _____ of its individual and corporate encounters with God.

- The church manifests a _____ _____ to God in renewed obedience to His known will.

- The church has an _____ _____ to revive other Christians and win the lost to Christ.

15. Some evangelicals today are certainly uneasy with the thoughts and conversations of revival because of what it historically _____.

16. **The Cycle of Revival:** The Spirit moves on a _____. The man becomes a _____. The movement becomes a _____. The machine becomes a _____ to a man. The Spirit moves on _____ man.

17. We must carry a sense of _____ for God along with a sense of _____ for our assignment.

The Distinctives of Revival

- An extraordinary work of God was differentiated and substantiated from the more _____, everyday work of the Holy Spirit in the life of the believer

- The acute awareness and realization of the unique and manifest presence of God was consistently reported in the _____ of the people.

- Revivals naturally tended to precede a significant _____ _____ and harvest of souls in the community that were touched by the *revived* church.

- Supernatural manifestations and demonstrations connected with revival and the outpouring of the Holy Spirit were _____ in Scripture.

18. Revival has always carried an unusual manifestation of God. Sometimes this is called _____ _____.

19. There must always be a demonstration of <u>fruit</u> for an experience to be labeled a New Testament revival.

20. Revivals have a much deeper and more significant impact upon the church than a mere display of the _____ *and* _____.

The Faces of Revival

- _____: Emphasis on "cleaning up" one's life

- _____: Emphasis on winning souls to Christ

- _____: Emphasis on magnifying God accompanied by a freedom of expression

- _____: Emphasis on experiencing God's indwelling

- _____: Emphasis on confronting and battling principalities and strongholds (religious, governmental, territorial and municipal)

- _____: Emphasis on supernatural occurrences (i.e. speaking in tongues, shaking, jerking, trembling, laughing, falling out, weeping, dancing, laughter, etc.)

- _____: Emphasis on physical and emotional healing and restoration

- _____: Emphasis on removal of religious/social division and injustice along with the proliferation and promotion of racial harmony

- _____: Emphasis on deliverance of personal bondage to sin and addiction and ongoing victory

- _____: Emphasis on the movement of intercession

21. It is not the face of the revival the makes the change. It is the _____ _____ that makes the impact.

22. The most important thing about a revival is _____ _____, not just experiencing its manifestations.

23. When revivals are all about manifestation, they become _____ and _____, sometimes even falling into the ranks of _____.

Creating Revival

24. The traditional view of revival is when a church invites a well-known or gifted _____ to *hold* a series of meetings focused on good preaching and soul winning.

25. True Revival is a _____ _____ of God upon a people.

26. _____ don't *schedule* revival. _____ schedules revival. Revival doesn't happen when an _____ visits a church. It happens when _____ visits a church

27. Just because we have initiated all the right parameters and set the stage, revival is not _____ to occur.

28. *Revivalism:* To add human _____ to create sensationalism for sensationalism sake.

29. Revivalism's ethos is _____ _____ and its methods are manipulative thereby creating a need for _____.

30. People who attempt to manufacture false phenomenon eventually end up _____ ____ _____.

31. Real revival sets a precedent that is hard to _____.

32. God needs no _____ _____. A true move of God ends up proving itself without man made _____.

33. Real revival is initiated and fortified by the Holy Spirit, the word of God, fervent prayer, and accountability to ecumenical council, whereby the Holy Spirit gives a _____ _____ to the glory of Christ.

34. Eventually true revivals lead to the evangelism of many souls by the _____ of the revivals themselves.

35. While it is true that a real revival is very disruptive to the traditional church, it only disrupts to the point where it puts the church _____ ____ ____ _____.

36. Revival is a _____ _____ to a _____ _____. It readjusts the church's priorities

37. The goal of true revivals is world evangelization and discipleship by means of the _____.

Seeking Revival

38. Sadly, many times revival doesn't occur because deep down some people don't really want to see revival unless it happens in _____ _____.

39. Before revival comes, God also moves on a man or a people in whom will *pray it through* to _____.

40. The church that Jesus died for should never coast but _____ to new heights.

41. None of the mandates given to us by Christ, to preach, reach, and teach can successfully occur without the _____ _____ of the Spirit.

42. For revival to start, we must be _____ by our own spiritual blindness, apathy, and pride.

43. The birthplace of any revival begins with the humbling of our own _____ _____.

The Cost of Revival

44. An all out revival of Holy Ghost proportions will cost a preacher his _____, his _____ and his _____ _____ of doing things.

45. The struggle with revival comes when a minister or a ministry is confronted with something that they didn't plan on or build their ministry around in the _____ _____.

46. A revival people insist that nothing is more important than God invading the _____.

47. The church in no way should operate without an _____ and _____ sense of power.

48. It is the responsibility of whomever God chooses to move through that they carry the move of God _____, _____, and _____.

49. Man's eternal quest is to _____, _____ and _____ God.

50. Though some may not admit it, they want God to quit playing _____ _____ _____ and show Himself.

51. Revival people are tired of _____.

For Discussion:

If seasons of extra ordinary and ongoing occurrences of supernatural activity cease, would the church be able to continue its mandate to win souls and make disciples on it's own *ordinary* power?

Would the church even dare accept *ordinary* as an option for it's operation? Did Jesus purchase the church and baptize it in the Holy Spirit for it to simply run on *neutral*?

Is it reasonable to assume and accept that the church can convert souls and disciple them by their own energy, without the much needed and increased enablement of the Holy Spirit and the demonstration of His power?

What makes the church the church? Is it the work of the people or is it the presence of God amongst the work of the people? What is deemed *enough* Spirit life and what is that measure?

Is the church operating with enough power to make its presence and influence known in the communities where they exist? Is *normal church* enough to fulfill the great commission?

Are we raising awareness of the authority and authenticity of Christ where we are?

Is it even appropriate to say that we don't need a sustained and incremental increase of revival among us? Are we full enough?

Is there enough availing of *Spirit life* in the church to carry on the work? Does *normal church* mean that the church then should be more of a social club *when* revival isn't occurring?

CHAPTER 18
Jesus is the Glory of God!

1. God's presence and glory on earth is _____!

2. At the end of the day our desire for the presence of God must _____ _____ the person of Christ.

3. Every great New Testament move of God, without exception, _____ _____ Jesus Christ.

4. Without understanding the Old Covenant revelation of worship, we truly can't truly appreciate and value the new covenant revelation of worship in the _____ ____ _____.

5. We must have a clear understanding that all the church does and all She stands for is to _____ and _____ Jesus.

6. We must replace the _____ _____ of the presence of God with JESUS!

7. So often we pine for, pray for and wait for the glory and yet, the true glory is _____ _____ ____.

8. Sometimes we whine for the glory as if it's an
_____ _____ _____.

9. The Bible says that the glory Moses experienced was
only a _____ _____.

10. The glory that the priests saw in the tabernacle once
per year was _____.

11. The glory that Solomon experienced at the dedication
of the temple that prevented the priests from entering
the temple was only a _____ _____ of the
true glory that has been revealed to us in Christ.

12. How can ministers lead people when they _____
_____ _____ what they are leading them to?

13. New Covenant leaders must focus on the _____
and _____ glory.

14. The visible revelation that is among us and remains is
<u>Christ</u>.

15. We must teach the church that we don't worship <u>for</u>
the presence. We worship _____ His presence:

16. Jesus is Emmanuel: God is _____ us.

17. Jesus is the _____ ___ _____, the _____, and the
_____ of the church.

18. In Revelation, Jesus is not knocking on the door of sinners; He is knocking on the door of the _____.

19. Jesus is the _____ _____ of the Father. When you've seen Jesus, You've seen God.

20. Sometimes in our pursuit of the presence of God we epitomize the things that _____ Christ, but never truly worship Christ.

21. Sometimes our worship is so _____ focused, _____ focused, _____ focused, _____ focused, _____ focused, etc.

22. There is no _____, _____ worship in Heaven. Every second of worship is a revelation of _____.

23. When Christ is the center of our worship, everything else takes on a _____ nature and _____ curiosity.

24. When Christ and His amazing grace are exalted, it creates a _____ _____ _____ and awe that cannot be described

25. Jesus pre-existed as a _____ Person from the Father and secondly, He _____ in His Father's glory before the world began – the _____ _____ of God's glory.

26. So often we pattern our worship services on _____ _____ ideals.

27. We must quit subliminally reenacting _____ _____ every time we gather as if there is a progression.

28. We no longer worship by patterns but by a _____.

29. Jesus is the _____ _____ of worship and ministry.

30. Through Christ we are _____ in God's presence. We don't have to work up a _____ to get there.

31. So often, in our fervor as leaders, we charge our congregations to love God with all their heart, yet _____ ____ _____ them that Christ first loves them.

32. Jesus came with a _____ _____ ____ _____. He redefined the way of love. *"In this is love, not that we loved God, but that He loved us."* (1 John 4:10)

33. Our love level for God _____ day by day. It rises and falls depending upon the _____ of our lives and our emotional love _____.

34. When you focus on your _____ and _____ for God, your zeal will eventually _____.

35. God doesn't love us because we are _____. He loves us because HE IS _____!

36. We need to turn everything over to Jesus and quit trying to run our ministries by our _____ _____ of thinking and doing things.

37. In order to have a _____ _____ with Him we have to let go of our agenda.

38. In a church where Jesus is the center of the picture, there will always be an _____ _____.

39. In a church where Jesus is the center of the picture, there will be constant _____ _____ and _____.

40. In a church where Jesus is the center of the picture, we will never lack for a _____ _____ of direction.

41. When Jesus is exalted in a church, it WILL be _____ _____.

42. When God's presence is recognized among us, His voice of _____ gives us power to be the church in our communities and cities.

43. When Jesus is lifted high in the church, God's love is _____ _____ in our hearts and we _____ the living Christ to all.

44. Keeping our eyes on Jesus is the true definition of
_____. It is how we keep everything we do in it's
proper _____.

45. All Presence-based ministry and activity totally focuses
on Christ and His _____ work!

For Discussion:

After studying this chapter how does your view of the presence
of God differ?

Have you ever been caught up in worship but felt that the
experience was somewhat ambiguous and confusing?

Does your leadership tend to put more emphasis in other aspects
of the worship other than Jesus?

Do the songs you sing for your worship services for the most part
exalt Christ and his finished work?

Is your church a candidate for a Jesus takeover? Why?

Discuss how you know that Jesus is the glory of God.

CHAPTER 19

A Leader That Lasts

---

1. You must know _____ you are and _____ you are

2. Ambitious leaders and selfish people have a way of trying to mold you into their image, put *Saul's armor* on you and make you something you're not in order to prevent you from making them _____.

3. Your value doesn't _____ based on someone's _____ to see your worth.

4. You are _____ to God!

5. Discovering who you are in Christ and who He is in you is the key to _____.

6. You are one of Heaven's top ranking emissaries. God has ordained you with His authority and sent you in His _____.

7. Satan doesn't break into _____ and _____ houses!

8. Confidence isn't _____ nor is insecurity _____!

9. The more _____ you are, the less confidence and trust you instill in others.

10. Don't project your _____ on others.

11. God gave ministers extra-sensitive _____ to read the atmosphere and discern secret, hidden things.

12. Most often people don't think _____ about you the way you think they do.

13. Don't allow the _____ of others to hold you captive.

14. If you don't believe in _____ no one else will.

15. Carry yourself in such a way that it doesn't invite _____ or _____.

16. When you open up to people's _____, they eventually throw hooks that land the _____ _____.

17. Never let anyone reduce you to a mere _____!

18. Never let anyone pressure you into _____ _____ no matter what, even if it costs you your position or reputation.

19. Don't compromise your _____ for the <u>approval</u> of people.

20. You are not an entertainer of _____ but an entertainer of _____.

21. You have what it _____!

22. God has given you your platform. Never _____ _____ yourself! Trust your God given gifts because God Himself trusts you.

23. Stop _____ yourself! Don't talk _____ about yourself. Use faith-filled and affirming self-talk. Use words that reflect what God _____, _____ and _____ about you.

24. When you change your _____ _____, you change everything.

25. If you don't believe in _____, how can you expect _____ to believe in you?

26. Never tolerate a _____ attitude or _____ from people. Carry yourself in such a way as to command _____ from others.

27. Your security and identity are in _____!

28. God always _____ your preaching, teaching, singing and leading. He is cheering you on and is extremely _____ of you, especially when you feel you've _____.

29. You have no idea how profound of an _____ you are having in the hearts of the people.

30. To God, there's no such thing as a _____ _____.

31. God never _____ you! He _____ you.

32. God does not take _____ of you like others.

33. Stop _____ and _____ about your progress! Put down the yardstick and quit measuring your value.

34. If you're going to obsess, obsess about _____.

35. You are _____!

36. God endorses you so no one else's _____ matters.

37. The anointing doesn't depend on how you _____ but in how you _____.

38. When you step out to run after God and do what He has commanded, _____ WILL happen.

39. Even your shadow has power because of the One who _____ You.

40. In order for God to preserves us for a special purpose He not only _____ us from familiar and

comfortable surroundings for a prescribed time, but also _____ us from venturing down the wrong paths.

41. A selfish leader isn't mindful of the things that _____ wants him to do. He is only mindful of the things _____ wants to do for God.

42. When God preserves a leader, He creates within him a _____ to withstand any environment and situation.

43. In order for you to produce lasting fruit, God must produce _____ as fruit.

44. Brokenness isn't brokenness until other people _____ your brokenness.

For Discussion:

What are the areas of your leadership where you struggle most? Do you feel these areas are impossible for God? Do you feel God has given up on you?

Do you see yourself as a high official, ambassador, or dignitary of Heaven? Do you see yourself of such great worth that the enemy is trying to break into and steal what God is doing in you and through you?

Do you tend to be the blunt end of people's jokes? Have you tolerated it because it makes you look humble? Have you been people's door matt? Are you ready to change this? What steps will you take?

Have you been spending too much time focusing on what YOU want to do for God instead of what HE wants you to do for Him? If so, what will you do about this?

On pages 269-276 what stage of the preserving process would you say you are in? Does this illustrations bring perspective to your life?

About The Author

For over 25 years Tony Sutherland has served on staff in the local church as well as traveled extensively around the world stirring in hearts everywhere a passion for God's presence and a powerful grace awakening through his music, teaching and preaching. Tony has captured the unique ability to effectively reach a wide diversity of people in today's church. His dynamic ministry style crosses denominational and cultural barriers impacting children, youth, young adult, middle age and seniors. Congregations large and small are refreshed by his passion for Jesus. Along with his busy traveling schedule, Tony serves on staff as a Worship Leader at Free Chapel's main campus in Gainesville, GA under the ministry of Pastor Jentezen Franklin.

Having over a quarter-century combined experience in various ministry areas including: worship, youth & children, church planting, associate pastoring, and an expansive itinerate ministry in evangelism and foreign missions (to name a few), Tony is well equipped to address the life of the local church on numerous levels. Along with these, he has also ministered in hundreds of established and thriving churches as well as young, church plants around the world, consulting a plethora of pastors from every size congregation, cultural background, denomination and Christ centered church movement. His extensive research and hands-on involvement in helping to develop church environments is an invaluable resource for growing ministries desiring to adopt an intentionally Spirit-led paradigm all based around the PRESENCE OF GOD.

Tony is also an accomplished songwriter having written songs with and for artists such as Israel Hougton, Micah Massey, Ricardo Sanchez, Ce Ce Winans, The Katinas, Mandisa, Phillips-Craig & Dean, Bishop Paul Morton, David & Nichole Binion, Ashmont Hill, Daryl Coley, Myron Butler, Ron Kenoly and many others.

Tony resides in the North Atlanta area with his beautiful wife Sherri of 24 years and their two amazing children, Anna Grace (12) and Asher (17).

Answers

CHAPTER 1 – A Presence-based Heart

1. miraculous, supernatural
2. body, Spirit-filled , gospel
3. see us, people
4. ignite us
5. celebrities, shepherds
6. man worship
7. great leader
8. famous, influence
9. achieves, conceives
10. unfeigned, unchallenged, unchanged
11. people
12. God's pleasure, humankind
13. more
14. embody, who, why
15. people, Jesus
16. formulas, fire
17. services, songs, series, programs
18. indivisible
19. passion, hunger, worship, prayer
20. one hour
21. beyond, borders, intimacy
22. shouts, whispers
23. intimately known
24. yesterday
25. another tent
26. Presence starvation
27. number one priority

CHAPTER 2 – The Presence-based Church

1. experienced
2. pleasant
3. grandparents, powerless

4. change, transformation
5. doing church, fresh encounter
6. epitomizes, superiority
7. presence, rejoice, grace, promotion
8. marching orders, orders filled
9. casual
10. permitted, prevented
11. smolder out
12. best condition
13. centrality, move
14. break out, shatter
15. small doses, undiluted
16. necessary
17. normal, unusual, speculation
18. offend
19. institutional walls, as needed
20. authenticity, existence
21. genuine
22. validate
23. willing

CHAPTER 3 – The Presence-based Culture

1. resistant
2. full display
3. proper place, priority
4. pitch, build
5. diffuse, apologize, console
6. permit, create
7. dictate
8. steeper, deeper
9. total control
10. understand
11. explain
12. expectation
13. accommodate
14. equivalent
15. console, adjust
16. fearlessly, stupor
17. clamor, commotion, noisy

18. fear
19. honored guest, owner
20. presence of God
21. properly worship
22. high enough
23. appreciation
24. sensitivity, dictate
25. live, thrive
26. climate
27. cool, cool
28. purpose
29. prosper, influence
30. tension
31. invite, around
32. ministry, transform
33. strength, own hand
34. limited
35. effortless favor
36. outside, inside
37. endorsement
38. manufacture
39. man, you

CHAPTER 4 – Characteristics of a Presence-based Church

1. survive
2. clarifies
3. Passion
4. Joy
5. Freedom
6. Victory
7. Power
8. Reverence
9. Revelation
10. Repentance
11. Holiness
12. Deliverance
13. Fascination
14. Restoration
15. Favor

16. Compassion
17. Justice
18. Protection
19. Peace

CHAPTER 5 – Our Need for the Anointing

1. recognize, steward
2. anointing
3. enablement, works
4. promote ourselves
5. crushed
6. fragrance
7. anointing
8. validate, Jesus' name
9. own advantage
10. bad for business
11. human initiative
12. who are we
13. heat
14. yoke of bondage
15. fatness
16. split second
17. herald, interpreter
18. same
19. seer
20. interpret, deliver, observation
21. mature
22. urgency
23. counsel of God
24. Discernment
25. faith
26. spontaneity
27. sabotaged
28. hosts
29. habitation
30. control
31. couriers

CHAPTER 6 – A Holy Ghost Outpouring

1. largest, fastest, growing
2. experience, skeptic
3. behind, drifting
4. place
5. new passion, inspiration
6. order, balance, prohibited
7. eliminated
8. detractor, drawing factor
9. distinguish, confirm, boldly
10. proof
11. promote, witness
12. fill
13. attractive, filled
14. imposters
15. inappropriate, outdated
16. full advantage
17. desperate demand
18. thirst, quench
19. remotely entertain
20. scorn, contempt
21. popularity, polarity
22. sign, gauge
23. failing methods
24. we use, uses us

CHAPTER 7 – Discerning the Excesses

1. disposition, attitude
2. integrity
3. make believe, pretend
4. affinity
5. adultery, relationship
6. discredit
7. signs, Jesus
8. central destination
9. inner witness
10. Word of God
11. discredit, destroy

12. interpreted, source
13. moving towards
14. demonic, familiar spirits
15. divert, deceived, distracted
16. real
17. placing signs
18. verification, exaltation
19. Word
20. real transformation
21. glorifies God
22. righteous source
23. discerning of spirits
24. gauged
25. disruptive, distracts, confusion, dread
26. external verification
27. edifies the church
28. beautiful harmony

CHAPTER 8 – The Last Days Church

1. rock stars, hit
2. popularity, stinging irritation
3. despise
4. futile, affection
5. denounce, deny
6. persecution, increase
7. modern day
8. signs, wonders, miracles, Spirit
9. sensitive seekers
10. validated
11. message
12. dumb down
13. coddle, cater, cave-in
14. discontent
15. sense, plan
16. resistance, rigidity, indifference
17. pioneering, landmarks, boundaries
18. mingles, resisting
19. fame, flame

20. trumpets, fury
21. honor, seek
22. younger, old
23. wise judgment
24. supernatural
25. earnest, down payment
26. performance, spiritual alarm
27. visible, brighter, shine
28. look, church
29. counsel
30. fundamental doctrines, released
31. salvations, discipleship
32. grace, worldwide
33. grace
34. prioritized, emphasized, epitomized
35. revival

CHAPTER 9 – The Personality Driven Church

1. servant leadership
2. discovered
3. celebrity showcase
4. shepherds
5. costly
6. fade into obscurity
7. sheep
8. walking the crowd
9. small
10. sacrifice
11. serve his needs
12. least, first
13. security
14. among men
15. hard wired, missing
16. as God
17. popular
18. Man made
19. little kings
20. pressure
21. sell yourself short

22. take credit
23. kindness
24. served, serve
25. iron fist, open hand
26. loyal, assets
27. leave you
28. poser, imposter
29. ones you have
30. unconditional, loving, reverence
31. commodity, community

CHAPTER 10 – Presence-based Leadership

1. bargain, stand bold
2. anvil of adversity
3. trust, truth, presence
4. broken, softened, remolded, Him
5. raising
6. small
7. famous
8. faithfulness
9. workout
10. Heaven's perspective
11. endure, ensure
12. process
13. endure
14. giants
15. recognition
16. shortcuts
17. exile
18. Location frustration
19. field, furnace
20. unfairly
21. hidden enemies
22. throw, over
23. blessing, lesson
24. devil
25. true
26. serve

27. difficult, humiliating, unappealing, harsh
28. circumcised
29. advantage
30. weakness
31. fear of man
32. entitlement
33. head

CHAPTER 11 – Performance-based Leadership

1. promotions, programs, parades
2. marvel, melt
3. captive
4. muse
5. amuse
6. undeniable
7. natural talent
8. betraying Jesus
9. technology
10. creator
11. counterfeit
12. demonic
13. sensitivity, integrity, love, grace
14. major, minor
15. novel, compromises
16. creativity
17. method
18. center
19. things, people
20. Jesus
21. market
22. old, new
23. pressured, intimidated
24. irritated, condemnation
25. indifference
26. Word of God
27. judgmental, genuine
28. outpouring
29. misunderstood, super spiritual

CHAPTER 12 – Image Driven Ministry

1. worldly mindset
2. Christ kingdom
3. glorious melting pot
4. old, fat, fashion
5. demographic
6. thin, suave
7. keep them involved
8. admired, respected, foremost
9. thrive together
10. generational, honor, respect
11. call of God
12. biceps, Bibles
13. insult
14. passion out positions
15. mental Photoshop, shine
16. trust Him, greater things
17. workout
18. positive influence
19. Young ministers
20. remove the hindrances
21. every age
22. wholeheartedly, never imagined
23. just ahead
24. you, He
25. all about Jesus

CHAPTER 13 – Confronting the 'Me' Monsters

1. integrity
2. character
3. small things
4. precious anointing
5. costs, hurts
6. climb, lowers
7. hungry, dragons
8. motives
9. success
10. press reports

11. big, small
12. opportunity away, for you
13. God alone
14. staggers
15. places, faces, spaces
16. stolen
17. promoted, humiliated
18. options, challenges
19. threatened, despised
20. dreams
21. silence
22. promotion
23. ready
24. possess
25. chase you
26. servants
27. anointed, feelings
28. preferences
29. honors
30. doormen
31. servant's quarters
32. feeling, choice
33. murdering spirit
34. Father
35. blinds
36. future
37. wisdom, unfairness
38. orchestrating
39. fruitful
40. poverty
41. favor
42. successes, hardships
43. God Himself
44. Inevitable
45. rejected, accepted
46. furnace of man's rejection
47. correction, protection, ejection, redirection, projection
48. removal, disapproval
49. launching pad

50. building blocks
51. greater

CHAPTER 14 – A Culture of Excellence

1. Excellence
2. slack, slack
3. higher
4. no less
5. slothfulness, laziness
6. best
7. disregarded
8. superior
9. Jesus
10. good, merit, quality
11. excel, more, cusp, resources
12. best
13. growing
14. inspires
15. represent
16. investment
17. wow
18. valued
19. glorious
20. embody
21. higher
22. church, take notice
23. drawn
24. average, ordinary
25. big
26. influence
27. quality
28. same type
29. following you
30. be the best
31. why, just good enough
32. whatever it takes, never good enough
33. character, competency, charisma
34. gifts, excellence, confidence, judgment, nature

35. endorsement
36. endorse
37. insufficiency
38. more, less

CHAPTER 15 – A People of One Thing

1. mile wide, inch deep
2. vision, pursuing, wrong thing
3. seek
4. watch, humble, seek, pray, repent
5. lookout
6. awareness
7. helpless
8. time allotted
9. first few moments
10. deviate
11. stupid, caught off guard
12. open
13. private space
14. pursue
15. actively, hope
16. music package, warm up
17. heart of man
18. life breath
19. desire
20. reveal, in line
21. repentance
22. change your mind
23. grovel, returning
24. believing, turning
25. perfect, repentant
26. stop, turn, return
27. comfortable
28. turning
29. attention, tension, nonexistent

CHAPTER 16 – The Vice Versus of Ministry

1. palatable, undiluted
2. options, people, face, earth, power, time, people, balance, people
3. God Himself
4. programmed, run through
5. face
6. selfish reasons
7. gifts
8. provision
9. forces of darkness
10. gimmicks, gadgets
11. money or men
12. apostolic power
13. wonders of old
14. time element
15. moment with God
16. generations
17. love, obedience
18. conservative
19. reach people
20. around
21. seeker, sought
22. preoccupation with God
23. worship rightly
24. remedied
25. sales pitches, oxygen tank
26. smile, change
27. Biblical illiteracy
28. PR facelift
29. refine confine, define
30. came, heard, left, did
31. possible scorn
32. press back

CHAPTER 17 – A Revival People

1. revival people
2. ongoing revival
3. normal

4. finished
5. passion, prayers, purpose
6. significant
7. conversion of souls
8. supernatural activity
9. harness, sustain
10. behind, within, in front of
11. cooperate, participate, navigate
12. continuous moving
13. results
14. resuscitating, once alive

Four Things that Happen to a Revived Church

    a. repents, intensely aware
    b. deepening
    c. positive response
    c. increased concern

15. costs
16. man, movement, machine, monument, another
17. urgency

The Distinctives of Revival

    a. ongoing
    b. testimonies
    c. evangelistic outreach
    c. confirmed

18. atmospheric revival
19. fruit
20. strange, unusual

The Faces of Revival

    a. Repentance
    b. Evangelism
    c. Worship
    c. Deeper Life
    e. Spiritual Warfare
    F. Manifestations
    g. Miracles
    h. Reconciliation

i. Deliverance

21. underlying power
22. knowing God
23. inclusive, sectarian, cultism

Creating Revival

24. evangelist
25. sovereign visitation
26. We, God, evangelist, God
27. guaranteed
28. manipulation
29. man centered, explanation
30. telling on themselves
31. refute
32. defense attorney, validation
33. great harvest
34. converts
35. back on its course
36. corrective measure, fruitful end
37. gospel

Seeking Revival

38. their church
39. fruition
40. catapult
41. supernormal
42. confronted
43. egotistical heart

The Cost of Revival

44. church, agenda, own way
45. first place
46. mundane
47. initial, sustained
48. faithfully, humbly, sensitively
49. know, experience, love
50. hide and seek
51. churchianity

CHAPTER 18 – Jesus is the Glory of God

1. Jesus
2. center around
3. always exalted
4. person of Christ
5. unveil, release
6. abstract concept
7. already among us
8. absent mystical notion
9. passing glory
10. transient
11. temporary reflection
12. don't even know
13. finished, final
14. Christ
15. from
16. with
17. All in All, center, essence
18. church
19. exact representation
20. surround
21. song, sign, wonder
22. pointless boring, wonder
23. marvelous, splendid
24. continuum of wonder
25. distinct, shared, full expression
26. Old Covenant
27. Tabernacle worship
28. Person
29. better way
30. already, lather
31. forget to remind
32. new way of love
33. diminishes, season, capacity
34. love, passion, deflate
35. loveable, Love
36. own way
37. fresh baptism
38. open Heaven

39. Spirit life, activity
40. clear voice
41. noised abroad
42. acceptance
43. shed abroad, reflect
44. balance, perspective
45. finished

CHAPTER 19 – A Leader that Lasts

1. who, Whose
2. uneasy
3. decrease, inability
4. valuable
5. everything
6. endorsement
7. worthless, empty
8. arrogance, humility
9. passive
10. insecurity
11. radars
12. negatively
13. expression
14. yourself
15. disrespect, contempt
16. jabs, big blows
17. entertainer
18. performance mentality
19. convictions, approval
20. men, angels
21. takes
22. second guess
23. belittling, down, thinks, feels, says
24. self image
25. yourself
26. demeaning, dishonor
27. Christ
28. flopped
29. impact

30. bad performance
31. evaluates, celebrates
32. inventory
33. assessing, obsessing
34. Jesus
35. anointed
36. opinion
37. feel, follow
38. miracles
39. overshadows
40. removes, prevents
41. God, he
42. resilience
43. you
44. see

Other Great Resources Available at
www.tonysutherland.com